UNREAL BUT REAL ANIMALS

EXTREMELY
BEAUTIFUL
CREATURES

by Megan Cooley Peterson

CAPSTONE PRESS
a capstone imprint

Published by Spark, an imprint of Capstone.
1710 Roe Crest Drive, North Mankato, Minnesota 56003
capstonepub.com

Library of Congress Cataloging-in-Publication Data is available on the Library of Congress website.
ISBN 9781666355239 (hardcover)
ISBN 9781666355246 (paperback)
ISBN 9781666355253 (ebook pdf)

Summary: Full-color photos and simple, engaging text describe a variety of beautiful animals, their habitats, food, and behaviors.

Image Credits
Getty Images: GlassEyeStock, 17, RibeirodosSantos, 29; Shutterstock: A. Storm Photography, 10, AB Photographic, 22, Agami Photo Agency, Cover (top), Alexey Seafarer, 21, Corrie Barbard, 12, Denis Vesely, 4, Ethan Daniels, 28, Hyserb, 23, Jan Hejda, 18, Klymenok Olena, 11, LILLIAN_GZ, 7, Makarova Viktoria, 15, Ogurtsov, 27, Oksana Maksymova, 28, RudiErnst, 5, scooperdigital, 13, Simun Ascic, 9, UniquePhotoArts, Cover (bottom), Vladimir Wrangle, 19, Zoltan Major, 25

Design Elements
Shutterstock: Cassel

Editorial Credits
Editor: Erika L. Shores; Designer: Hilary Wacholz; Media Researcher: Pam Mitsakos and Jo Miller; Production Specialist: Tori Abraham

All internet sites appearing in back matter were available and accurate when this book was sent to press.

TABLE OF CONTENTS

Words in **bold** are in the glossary.

NATURE'S SHOW-OFFS

Big eyes. Soft fur. Flashy feathers and scales. The animals in this book are nature's show-offs. They turn heads wherever they go. But their beauty is more than just for looks. It helps these cute creatures stay safe and find food.

BEAUTY IN THE AIR

DRESSED UP

A group of peafowl is called a party. And these fancy birds are dressed for fun. Males have bright blue heads. Feathers on their backs can grow 5 feet (1.5 meters) long. Males fan out their long feathers to find a female. Eyespots on their feathers seem to dance.

FACT
Female peafowl are called peahens. Males are called peacocks.

DASHING DUCKS

Male mandarin ducks look like living artwork. Their feathers have dashes of white and black. Blue, green, purple, and orange feathers almost glow.

Mandarin ducks build nests high up in trees. Females lay nine to 12 eggs at a time. Ducklings must jump out of the tree to find water.

FLYING GLASS

Is that a piece of flying glass?
A glasswing butterfly has clear wings.
Light passes through them. Tiny hairs
grow on the see-through wings. These
hairs keep their wings from **shimmering**.
Hungry birds can't see them.

FANCY FACE

With its long eyelashes, the secretary bird has a face made for movies. But don't let its good looks fool you. These African birds are deadly hunters. They work in pairs to chase food. They peck at snakes, insects, and small **mammals** with their sharp bills.

BEAUTY ON THE GROUND

FAIRY TAILS

Friesian horses look like they galloped out of a fairytale. These horses have shiny black coats. Their long, flowing tails and **manes** blow in the breeze. Friesians can weigh more than 1,400 pounds (635 kilograms).

FACT
Friesian horses have starred in many movies and TV shows.

FEELING BLUE?

Peacock parachute spiders make other tarantulas seem dull. **Neon** blue hairs grow on their legs and body. Small patches of yellow sprout from their knees. They also have deadly **venom**. A bite from this beauty can cause humans pain for days.

FACT

Peacock parachute spiders live in only one small area in India. Not many remain in the wild.

STRIKING STRIPES

Night falls. An Amur tiger slinks through tall grasses. It hunts a deer. The tiger's orange fur has black and white stripes. These stripes break up the outline of its body. The deer can't see the big cat. Then the Amur tiger attacks.

FACT

Amur tigers can weigh more than 600 pounds (272 kg). They are the largest of all big cats.

LET IT SNOW

Arctic foxes get dressed up for winter. In fall, their brown fur starts to turn white. Blending in with the snow keeps them safe. It also helps them hunt. They dash through the snow without being seen.

FACT
Arctic foxes sometimes follow polar bears and eat their leftovers.

TREE MASTERS

What animal looks like a cross between a bear and a raccoon? The red panda! They have round, fuzzy faces and big ears. Red pandas climb trees. A bushy tail helps them balance.

FACT
Red pandas live near giant pandas. They both eat bamboo. But these animals are not related.

PRETTY BUT SMELLY

Not every beautiful animal is furry. Some are scaly. The San Francisco garter snake has stripes of bright blue, black, and red scales. These snakes aren't a danger to people. But don't get too close. They let out a gross smell when they get scared.

BEAUTY IN THE WATER

FEATHERY ARMS

A dazzling animal lives in the ocean. The feather star moves its feather-like arms up and down. It slowly sinks onto a **coral reef**. Tiny **plankton** get stuck in the feather star's arms. Then the feather star eats.

FACT
Heavy feather stars can't swim. They walk along the ocean floor.

COOL CRABS

Does candy walk? It does if it's a candy crab. This crab's body has swirls of pink and white. Candy crabs blend in with the coral they call home. These tiny crabs are only a little over 1 inch (2.54 centimeters) long. Their small size helps them hide from attackers.

GLOSSARY

coral reef (KOR-uhl REEF)—a type of land made up of the hardened bodies of corals; corals are small, colorful sea creatures

mammal (MAM-uhl)—a warm-blooded animal that breathes air; mammals have hair or fur; female mammals feed milk to their young

mane (MAYN)—long, thick hair that grows on the head and neck of some animals like lions and horses

neon (NEE-on)—extremely bright

plankton (PLANGK-tuhn)—tiny plants and animals that drift in the sea

shimmer (SHIM-ur)—to shine or sparkle

venom (VEN-uhm)—a poisonous liquid produced by some animals

READ MORE

Arnosky, Jim. *Look at Me!: Wild Animal Show-offs*.
New York: Sterling Children's Books, 2018.

Emminizer, Theresa. *Fantastic Arctic Foxes*.
New York: PowerKids Press, 2022.

Hofer, Charles C. *Adorable but Deadly Creatures*.
North Mankato, MN: Capstone Press, 2022.

INTERNET SITES

Arctic Fox
worldwildlife.org/species/arctic-fox

Indian Peafowl
kids.nationalgeographic.com/animals/birds/facts/
indian-peafowl

Secretary Bird
kids.sandiegozoowildlifealliance.org/animals/
secretary-bird

INDEX

ABOUT THE AUTHOR

Megan Cooley Peterson has been an avid reader and writer since she was a little girl. She has written nonfiction children's books about topics ranging from urban legends to gross animal facts. She lives in Minnesota with her husband and daughter.